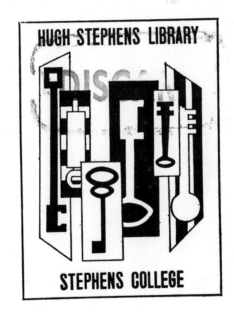

A Beginning

THE BEGINNING IS NOT MERELY HALF
OF THE WHOLE BUT REACHES OUT TOWARD
THE END.

ARISTOTLE, *Ethics*

A Beginning

POEMS

by William Burford

NEW YORK

W · W · NORTON & COMPANY · INC ·

Contents

A Beginning

From Within

These people are death, and we have only life.
They watch us in our extravagance—
No more for us than life—

A secret reserve, a glory deeply quiet,
Work, writing, and to eat the shared food,
Meeting and parting then as we do,
One car, older now, like its owner
And your bicycle, blue I think
As the sky we live under.

But precisely this is our triumph,
This measureless privacy;
Yet near to us is a curious neck
Ready to peck savagely, and make
Mess of our deep taste.

"These people are life, and have we only ourselves?"
I answer that, and tell you,
Your youthful demanding eyes,
That the self is strong, unisolated,
And from its birth forms bonds throughout all.

Before the Federal Building

No man could shoot through that
Gray solar glass almost black
And an inch thick up where he is
At the top. Even the sun's shafts
Are blunted, turned back—
  Or into an illusory atmosphere
  Where his face has a religious tinge.

Must we be mad to want to blast?
To think the clear ones should be our rulers
Who can stand in the day's light, valuable
Even in their wounds and worst chance,
Their bare, bloodied heads.

But the camouflaged men, the fish
Who look out at us from a hard bubble,
Or from under a brim always there—
If law will not let us touch them,
Yet sense cannot be taught they must win,
  Hypnotizing existence.

Barcelona
(*Summers of '36, '65*)

There are no more Barcelonas, like that one. And think, also,
It was but a month—July, into August—a great
Unselfishness swept men. Now almost thirty years ago.

Why do I tell you this? Because power, at the heart,
Infests every avenue and counts the hours
Until it wins. You study law: Are we not relentless?

In that city where I never went, as you did,
(Not knowing it would be our true place of all)
Was your back against that wall scarred with pits

At the cemetery from which the sea is visible,
As if, though yet unborn, you were shot when you saw?
And I a boy, who cut out pictures once of a war.

How shall we meet? How come together, across
The real space before that wall? Except naked,
Powerless, as men are, who have to start.

Histories

I *The Land of Learning*
Before noon, savage masks,
Shadows of lanterns on the Colleges,
Of iron lamps upraised at the doors—

Like the great blind cast there,
The unknowing king beaten by the light,
The pitiless prongs, that make the dumb wise—
Shade with dark laurels raised on the walls.

Crowns of thorn.

Uttered within, the human word
Tells what life is, its mounting forms—
With those cries suddenly heard
Like an animal killed or fowl,
That have our sound,
Before thought shapes the words—
Under the sky, the sun in its course.

II *The Brain*
A king, lifted on its own clear eloquence,
An island in the sea— But before, and afterward,
The gray brain in the jar, dull and unspeaking:

Lost, sunk into slough, prodded by returning devils
With pikes to hear it utter what remorse or agony it feels;
Then left, lying mute at last on the bank:

Where like a stone, a huddled animal, it moves
Slowly back to life, containing in itself

The transforming history of its own birth, and seeming
    death,

And restoration.

III *The Balloon*
    And afterward, on the third day,
    We found the empty skin, in a field where it lay,
    Blowing there in the early morning wind—

Like a specter, it rose from the mine shaft,
Emerged, slipping free, with its long shroud
Flowing round it, like a great jellyfish,
And ascended from earth into the stratosphere,
Where was its home, where it passed beyond men's sight,
Drifting upward, through the day and night of space,
The violet band, the deepening shades, and blackness,
Through which a sun of unimaginable light waited.

IV *Legend*
And had he come out of the opaque pool
The dark marsh pierced first by shoots
There at his foot; And could make, given it,
Only his own life, however immense the sun
He looked up at, however flashing the sea—

Not to lose it was the instinctive knowledge
He grasped to him: Until in time, a sense
Of happiness denied, a spreading sadness,

Inexorable lack, drove him savagely back
Wielding the self-murdering weapons.

The last assault remembers the beginning—
Was happiness there, in that world he first saw?
Those sunlit beaches he had grown divided from?
Let the new heroes bring this in their hands,
On their open palms, disarming freshness!
A visible substance, yet like air, like our breath.

The future? it was the beginning

Even as we looked at it
As I showed you its earthly shapes
"Like the face of Adam raised
By God's hand out of dust"
As the maker of the glass
Gave the molten grains
The flowing sand our likeness.

The truth was— I sought example
For some perfect touch, passion
And clarity at once,
Not seduction, not music,
Not a blind plunge down to depths,
But open eyed, an instruction,
Toward the manly, future world.

What if a certain dumbness
All creatures have, marks us,
If mind cannot entirely glance,
Or feeling turns back to greed
Like a tough root? Still I live
In the promised future
Of your face, alert, firm,

Out of the dark glass looking,
The vitreous shadows,
Out of the fire like a veil—
And think to take it with my hand
When I have skill enough,
Or you yourself instruct me
By clearest willingness.

16

Space

I

In the air, instruments circle—ours, theirs,
Recording, signaling the world.
But at heart we do not care;
These wonders turn ordinary.

But it is in our hearts that we are lost
Or spared—for a minute searching
Each other's faces,
The instruments traveling there;

Appearing and fading, as this
Were space, were night and pale day.

II

Yet are we destined
To find another face,
A skin different from
Any known in this place?

Are we bound outward,
Not more deeply within,
Or are both ways the same?
As yet, we see only

Those pocked surfaces,
Far less fair than earth—
Dusts blown desolately,
A crust. But are these rinds,

This utter ugliness,
The beginning of a tale
Whose promise is: We shall find
That beauty in the end we trace?

The Second City

This is the City of Man,
Who kills—And eats the animals
Given to him still,
Though now, through the city's extent,
They are almost invisible.

But the Opera's chandelier,
Faceted crystal glittering,
Is hung all dripping still
As if risen from the bloody pool,
Though white and clear.

But here are the black, earth mills,
And here the smoking air,
Where the pure wafer falls
Like snow or blossoms
On a million waiting mouths.

The millions look up at the buildings—
You will live there, and not die—
The whisper is given
From the city's heights—
Raised out of the ground

And not sent back,
Like that sheer element, glass,
And bronze unperishing,
But then shadowed, dark cast:
Towers of reflection

Upon the earth they came from,
Left by their mortal architects;

Who build a vast Memorial
The millions walk among
Seeking immortal life

That secret of all design:
As in that luminous picture
Where the people stand in profile
Like stone on the green bank
As though in eternity

Their animals with them,
A black dog with the nose
Of a hunter scenting,
And the water rippling near their feet—
That the City for all to look keeps.

Lines

The moon, torn from earth's side?
Like a rending of flesh and propelled,
Leaving the rushing ocean, and ourselves
At its edge.

Above, we've seen it looking broken
On the clouds, listing, shipwrecked
(But not as here), a strange fragment

Drifting, only half itself. What link
Could draw it in? Or is the distance kept
That we may see it grow enormous again

And know how wholly lost to us it is,
Even now, as it appears
Over the rim, as we hurl out lines

To it—as harpooners would—
Whose heart is blood and huge within
That white skin, we would crawl (like men) over

Encircling it again.

The Oaks

In the day I saw them, the dog
Who hunted, and the raucous birds,
The squirrel come to be fed
From the hand of the nun,
And always the trees' dark trunks—

Through whom we speak and lift our tongues.

At night the white moon, risen once more,
Sweeps over us like nakedness
Of one known without words,
To whom we go, pale body freckled with dust,
Through the black oaks—

Luminous, like bread before it is touched.

Nuns at an Airfield

I
Black-robed those Muses,
Watching the long planes
That rise up slowly
On smoking wings

II
They themselves, in their
Flaming robes, winged headdresses,
Holding the rail at the edge
Of the great world of air—
Almost ascend
On the rushing wind
They stand against
With ecstatic faces,
Bright cheeked, partaking
Of the Creation
Which destroys and makes,
Burning, propelled by
Its fuels and luminous saints,
These ships of the fleet.

I Know Not the Man

In Paris, city of light—

My ghost, who had made the journey
Of the city's long and glaring street,

Returned tonight and stood facing me,
Poor devil I was ashamed to be

And did with all my life deny,
Measuring the seven feet of walk that climbed

Between us, concrete, and the curb
Falling to the chasm where he burned

And to me cried, "Are you and I
Not halves? Pull me from the fire.

Give me your hand." I sat and watched him
Sink before my eyes, until extinguished.

At which instant there did rise
A shining figure of gold, that by

Its burning had been so turned.
"It is you!" then I cried— But went unheard

In that city, as day rose.

Twenty-year-old Poet

I

To Amsterdam,
Forty-nine islands
Shaped like a fan,
Or scythe—from the map
It struck his mind—
He came, that spring,
Sensing the flesh of all things
As the train swept by.

The black locomotive,
Brass veins combed back
And the smoking hide,
Passed stations on the way
With cry like the slain,
Whose white bones were laid
As speechless stones
Marking the flower beds.

And the lovely meadows
Of the Netherlands
Lay half in ashes—
Where the salt sea crawled,
Scaly and gray,
Steam shovels lifted up
The infernal rust
Which sifted from their jaws.

The city itself
Was a silent place;
Hosts of people
Drifted cycling by

With ghostly motion
Like birds in the sky.
Only when it rained
Was anything heard.

Then on the pavement,
Toward evening time,
The thin tires made
A sound of wailing,
Continuous, shrill,
Like winding tape
Being stripped away
From the great King of the Dead.

II
And she came in like Spring
Her light hair blown
And skin of lucent pearl—
"At night, you can see"
The whores in picture windows
Skirts hitched up to their naked thighs
In the licking light.

Inside at dinner they drank the Dutch gin
And he listened to the older men:
"What raises us above the beasts
Is our will. To live is to persist."
Words of the wise lens-grinder
Who lived in this Amsterdam
Where the bitter man sat
With malice in his grin:

"But the will will break"
He struck the board with clawlike hand.
"And purpose not last past twenty-five.
"A man drag back where he began and die."

He stared at me with dilated eye,
And he drew closer, in the smoke
And drunken din that filled that dive.

III
What comfort, then, can a man find?
Good friend, let us walk a while
Together. It is night. The fog is in.
The sea air is chill. There is no sign of life.

From far down the street
Shone a light like a star,
But the rays were cold
And did not reach
To warm the heart.
In all that world
The only thing heard
Was our own echoing feet

Approaching the place
Where the paving stone
Broke off in empty space—
The Museum loomed up
In whose cavernous rooms
Christ's body lies
For the dissecting knives.
And the stumps of the trees

Confronted us,
Monstrous teeth
Breaking through from beneath.
We reached the canal
Where the black water ran
And the barge at the bank
Lay huge and still
As the funeral bier.

"Here we must part, and not fear.
"Clasp hands. Pledge eyes."
And he gave me manly blessing.
Then he turned. But I
Stood and watched on that bank
The living coal of his pipe
Glow through the engulfing night.

From the Ground
(Harper's Ferry)

I am Newby:
Three days long
In the street of the town
My black body lay,
Rooted by the sows.

I, Thompson:
Under the bridge
In trickling water
My face gazed dumbly,
Shot and flung down.

I, young Oliver Brown,
The youngest one, the boy,
Lay in my blood on the floor
Where nothing more could help me,
And did not die until dawn.

Ossawatomie, I,
In whom the living God—
Held my head upright
Until hung at Charles Town,
In my hooded crown.

Lawrence/ Ross/ Shaw

Unlike the lizard, that could shed his skin,
Wherever he fled, still it went with him;
Was the tent he rose and lay down in,
Stretched by his own frame, his tendons
That clenched or gave, as the world would penetrate
With soothing waters or stinging whips.

His actions could imitate other men's,
But he was not one of them;
He lived, instead, with an animal's sense,
With elaborate disguise, like women.
In heaven, if we can imagine him,
He reached some sphere of the English angelic,
Where white men their dark protectors kiss,
Exchanging earthly destinies, as he wished.

Inner and Outer

I *The Wind*
Over the land, chatter
Of Critics, Experts, Analysts,
A swarm of them, a whole class,
All that common terminology
In half-intelligent mouths—

Turns to gibberish,
Mixes in a twister
Of rattling syllables,
Of little sticks,
In a world of opinions
Where one churns indistinctly out
As another rushes in.

Wind or gutter,
Whichever you will.

II *The Mind*
By degrees the mind can grow
Too familiar with itself;
Speak the same words,
Make the gestures it made before,
And commit a kind of incest
In the silver mirror—

A man must smash, break to bits,
Or with better wisdom, turn from,
Having gazed long enough
At that ghost, past its time.

III *The Students*
The god of Love sits brooding:
He is a student in a temporary room.
What should he do? What pursuit follow?
Simply to love would end in nothing.

But beautiful face and beautiful body,
How can they believe in school,
Or learn less than their own good?
This is not vanity. It is truth—

Longing for the book of books,
In which they can read themselves;
And given that evidence, go
Like the wise man, who was ugly,
    And taught them their souls.

Local God

There stands a man in Round Rock
Can grasp the rattlers behind the head
And snap them like a whip
Cracking their coiling backs.

He is the God of these hissing snakes;
Milks the venom out of their mouths
And wraps them round his arms like bracelets.

He is our chief scientist: savage and delicate.

Poem for a Daughter

On the child's, the stripling girl's,
My child's, my six-year-old's,
Fragile shoulder bones—
I touch them, I know—
Like a fledgling bird,
What crimes will I load,
Her father, breaking her!

Yet, it shall not be so!
Loving, I can save her,
Though what we've been is known.
Then somewhere far I'll not hear
The child crying from earth,
Estranged, cast out, alone.
Now here, I will simply work for her.

The Sea Lavender
  for Denise Levertov

I

Shines at the world's edge,
Blown by the thin air,
But holding, rooted there
In its swept and else
Barren element.

Its lavender bloom
And gray leaf's hue
Make it a thing fair,
Which keeps that place,
That desolate station

With secret gladness.

II

Inside, in the glassy bowl,
All winter its resonant shadow
Like ocean shone;

Flashed and darkened
Beneath its branches
Like a thing passionate,

An animal spirit gathered,
On the mantel
An upreaching flame.

The Climbers

I *The Valley*
High, over the ranges, its cone in blue air as though floating,
The white mountain, the unmoving silence, shines.

We wait, knowing it is there. We delay the time:

Below, in the green valleys, by the streams and the flowers
Like foam hanging. From the meadows we hear the bells
Tinkling clear as dew. We dream; we turn back our minds.

Like hives of bees the prayerwheels hum perpetually,
And to the wind we give our days, reading fates,
Signals in the twig, the fluttering silk.

At night comes sleep, rustlings of snow, blue crevasses
Opening. Almost, we do not have to go;
Almost can stay, and still know that white world.

II *The Ascent*
But one morning, rising early, without word we set out.
We move forward. We see the earth rise in terraces before us.
We do not linger. We climb steadily. At the last village,
As we pass there, they look at us without expression.
The world grows barer. We reach the end of vegetation,
The line dividing living things from dead: the glaring ice.

We pause, then. On our faces we smear the pale ghostly
     masks.
At that light our eyes can only look by dark lens glass;

And what we see, what reach, in that cold kingdom where
    we go

    Is receding mystery.

III *The Plume*
Beautiful, where it blows there on the roof of the world,
The white, snow plume. Perpetual wind streams there

On the peak, where like the slow rising shape from the deep
We see it spray; and through the veil, glimpse the face

That haunts our sleep, that does not move.

IV *The Lhoste Face*
Stony, sheer, crisscrossed by icy scars, almost obliterated,
Like a huge slate, with the scrawl on it, tilted blindly up—

Of men that fall, of men whose dreams it follows,
Coal blue, cloudless at that altitude,
Could it know, and draw them
Like a great mirror to their souls
Round the world, finally to it?

The Spell

You can almost see him, looking as if well,
Shedding it, shaking it off,
The least shadow on the shoulders
Marking the hurt—as if absorbed almost;
Then the face turning, alive—

Only hesitating momentarily—

Until you remember how the head
Was horribly shattered
And fell, with the lifted hair,
As from an ax in back—Oswald
Cutting a path for himself
In the midst of America, a wedge;

But was the thing as it sped,
Coppered, leaden, not stopped
Perhaps there in the invincible thick hair?
Where the woman with her skill
Could pick it away, in her lap,
Breaking the spell? in the cloth of her dress—

It was deeper than that;
Neither burr nor dune thistle,
Nor like the roses she held
Black as blood in the light, so dark red—
But a kind of blunt bud, splintered
Into flower, that could not be touched,
Having its own final force that spread throughout,
The blind dark overwhelming him.

The Days of Love
  for my wife

I
How longer hold this division?

Though all things grow, by gradual
Unfolding with the days—

Now I see
Like shadow through the skin
Of your smooth temple,
Tracery of veins
Bearing the heart's beat,
The dark tree of your being:

And sense—
My own blood beating
(Pulse speaking almost to pulse)
In this same mortal place
That stones can break—
How thin is the division
Which holds the one life here,
And the other, there beyond touch.

II
Trellis of the veins the quick leafed blood climbs
And the birds there thronged with open throats sing,
Green, gold, rising—structure of a dream
Love in sleep reveals;
                    And then to wake,
Half awake, as smiling the vision fades,
The god takes leave, in the fragrant morning.

III

As for the world of things
That fill the space between us:
The Bed; Book; Arm of the chair—
Flesh almost of the room—
Each thing must teach us
That we are elsewhere,
Not to be held.

Life is motion,
Is air, blue sky—

But by an hour's time,
The day itself divided,
Shadow of branches
So fall across the path
That the heart cries out
Feeling your absence,
As my very life cut.

IV

Always, at first, I cannot look at you,
When you return—days gone—to this room.
You lie down on the bed and shut your eyes.
It is early morning. The world is quiet:

Down the long streets by which you come.

Nor do I either ask, or speak,
But lie there still beside you;
Knowing, only, the rise and fall
Of your being, as you breathe.

The Centaur

So he, whose legs were stunted, drew the legs
Of his father's racing horses, their knees
Like rocks, their hooves hurling dust;
Or on the box above his four-in-hand harnessed,
The Count himself driving, with white beard,
A fantastic figure buttoned up to the chin
In a coachman's outfit, with cape flowing—
Lautrec and the real coachman sitting in the rear,
Behind the charging horses, their legs like forearms bent;

That would turn in time into the bicyclers,
The racers with tendoned calves and thighs;
And in succession, the negro dancer in checkered pants
Pointing with his toe, almost a balletic step;
And the greedy one, so called, her hair built up
Into a sort of horn on top of her head
While she did a kicking dance, crooking her leg;
And last of all, standing still for him,
With an empty look, the prostitutes, in loose hose.

After twenty years, nearly at the end,
Still seeing plainly, though his eyes were narrower now,
Half open on the pillow, he saw him trying
To switch the flies away with a strip of elastic tape
From his son's death bed, flicking it overhead;
And looking up, not without mercy he said
"Must you always be such a silly fool?"
And then said nothing more:
Himself a poor figure of another sort

Who lay there, half covered, sweating above the sheet
In the heat of September, as though the brothel
Had become a hothouse. Sinking now, closing

His eyes finally, taking the pictures inward,
He entered then a state of troubled dream,
A slight frown upon the brows, as in that sketch
Of the girl asleep but not wholly peaceful,
Still coping in her mind with what she has met,
No less than the reality of life, her life,

And also his who watched her, unresting,
Not yet released to either sleep or death—
To the mother who had borne her once,
And his mother, whom he painted, sitting, her hands
Beside a cup, in the sun room of her house,
Where he had come back to die;
Who would gather all his pictures at last,
Long after his strange father, who played
His part in them, had returned to the chase.

A Reply

No, Lowell, their hair was not Botticellian and golden,
Nor did they comb it like girls, one the other's,
Those three hundred, before they advanced to die
At Thermopylae. They were all men in middle age,
Fathers of sons, chosen by Leonidas with sober reason.

This was no American high-school football field
Of the nineteen-sixties where boys with blond hair
Worn long in the style now, nearly become lovers
While the whole body of fascinated citizenry shudders.
These forty-year-old soldiers hardly moved onto the plain

Like Aphrodite. Would you be curious as that Persian spy
Who described their habits to Xerxes, amazed, half
Prurient? Or were you thinking of the slender young
Sons of Priam in Homer's story who one by one
Ran before pitiless Achilles who killed them

Though they grasped his knees and looked up?
No, Lowell, look at yourself, middle aged, your grisled hair
Half taken, and think of what beauty this time of life
Can possess. Men try to offer themselves cleanly
To their deeds, even to death, on the last surrounded hill

   Past any habit of embellishment then.
   Look at what all of us must become.
   "Glittering with liberation?" No,
   Or only within, holding, self-contained,
   Perhaps dust-covered, sweating, in
   Rivulets, shining through that, if
   We're to imagine how they ended.

Cypris, Athene

This afternoon, black, green, and gold,
An effect of hair, of clothes, were your
Shield, your spear. Yes, my eyes feared:
I could tell the torso, the curving stream
To be seized by one who could win,
To be plundered. We were moving closer, meshing,
But still the laughter parrying, the white teeth,
The wave in foam
                    blood swelling, rushing below,
The veil enveloping, tearing—

After possession, is loving knowledge perhaps,
Touching those wounded places our hands
Made on the flesh—covering them;
Looking up now for a while at least
No longer into risk: with mild eyes
And now still lips.

The Museum

After the shattered athlete-god, the torso like a great ash
Held up on its rod, and one after one across the room
Fragments of a foaming wave gone—was the Bodhisattva in
    repose,
Having their almond eyes, the head with that smile, but the
    legs folded
Under him like flower stems, the mud-born lotus man—
    Alexander
Come into India!—where the wave ended in this god, sitting
    still,
Having absorbed them into its secret parts, where it was
    joined,
The ashes, the fragments, all floating to it, the final whore,
Who sat with them now, distant, knowing her mystery.
Only the living Apollo might have outfaced her, but he was
    gone,
Not wanting to see himself in this form, under these veiled
    eyes.

The Dance

I

The pursuit of beauty is filled with living bodies;
Those left behind are as if dead, though they may rise again.

The pursuit is pressed through apparitions, reaching
For the ever living one, farther, more intensely.

It is pitiless, casting off, refusing, stripping itself
Even for its own end, when for that instant, beauty is held,

Which is another self, trembling, which in our hands, falls
    back.
There is no endless possession, only birth and death

As long as we have the strength to seek them again.

II

See that aging face—Once a dancer itself, now the Master
Of these who dance—on which the shadow, the anguish
Of the actual end is cast, implacable, the ashen
Valley into which he must descend, like the real
Enacter of some myth he invented to dance, as if
The hammer with which in a symbol he built the dance,
Upright in his grasp, turned and were battering him back—
So that face, dented, beginning to hollow, would say.

Yet there is still great grace! And is the process slower,
Gentler, than that hammering attack? Is it as though
A net were drawing him in, him alone, while all else
Ran, slipped past, so fair they were still,
These long stemmed girls that made his garden, that waved

With wind, with currents, and he the dying Master amidst
The buds of their breasts and the boys' round groins.
Now over them all he sees the invisible huge net,

Suspended there, neither rising nor coming down, set in the
        air:
Setting the limit they leap against, not knowing it,
Breathless with oblivion. They move like a wave with fishes
Held springing there before him; that ceases, so that he sees
Their deep breaths. They have a long time still. Only he
Is being gathered by the invisible, descending net—
Which is there, traced in his own face staring,
Before it is covered, not a mask yet, looking for space.

The One Dancing

They speak of a seamless voice,
Unseen the flesh that projects it
Though felt to be there, invisibly singing—

Yet what of a body that itself
Is flawless, moving smooth as a deer,
That rose as if the air were water, as if slowly,

And then repeated this again
Without a step between, so it appears—
Yet all happening with a miraculous speed,

In leaps. He stops suddenly
And stands revealed to us, still,
His life breathing in the perfect skin he wears,

The flowing surface molded
Over the hips' round stones
And the genitals here innocent of their sex—

Into one form unbroken
Drawing upward toward the neck,
And there his head, the first thing mortal,

Yet hardly knowing danger,
Holding the perfect modesty
Of his stance, as if this were a talisman

Against that force, masked,
Destructive, waiting in the wings
To tear him away from his own completeness.

The Gypsy

Too late for the gypsy funeral, the extravagant
Wailing of that ancient race, the bangles
Clashing on the wrists, for the dead prince—
The passion perhaps not true any more.
And I knew, then, in the empty church
Whose windows shone with a light neither warm
Nor cold, abandonment of a different sort.

Could the spirit be injured to the core?
Beyond lament, beyond natural return?
The person within so harmed and stunned
It could not lift? Along the vault above,
Strange architecture that puzzled my sight,
There was a rod or bar, of dark mahogany,
More than ornament it seemed, like a hand grip

Or for the chin or teeth, or locked to the oar—
This an instrument of bloody heart-ribbed rack,
But so high it was immaculate, not dripping
Either sweat or blood; and the eye fell
To the station where the image of us all
Was on hands and knees, trying to crawl.
The church's walls were calm. They rose upward

To that untouched and unmoving rod.
What was it? Justice, Law, the form
That Love takes even as He watches
The anguish of His own blood; as He weeps
Tears not seen on the grain of that bar.
The father is no gypsy, and he answers none.
The son must know this, go to his own fate.

A Face

There was no secret in those eyes,
Though they were the eyes perhaps
Of some god.

What they offered was a hard ground
Desire would waste itself upon.

Like that ground I saw also
In New Mexico in a dry pueblo yard,
Grassless, packed down, like clay or stone
The sudden rain swept and ran off
Leaving it as before.

In the mountains were the gods,
Of snow, of dark fir, of cloud.

This was the bare face
Without imprint, I looked on,
Or change of fate.

Going to School

By science comes everything. It offers a future
To you, like a jewel— So your mother gives you,
White, made of ivory and bamboo, marvelously smooth,
A slide rule, a magic instrument you take in your hands—

That moves and grows, out of itself, but ever
Returns again perfectly true. It makes you
A kind of god as you work it; and at times
When the crystal viewer magnifies its red lines
It is like a ruby you have. It hangs at your side
In its leather case against your thigh; it has become
A part of you, as it were almost your very life.
You can tell its weight on your belt, its presence
Along the flesh of your leg, to which it gives a strength
As you step. On your birthday, from some impulse
Or signal your nature makes, you buy a charm, a silver
Elephant on a link, to hang from the case, and signify.
Your legs have grown strong and solid around. You are like
A young elephant, a royal one, or an elephant
In the form of a prince; and the pale washed jeans you wear
Seem to be your blue skin, like Vishnu's, in one of his shapes,
Who held up a mountain on the palm of his hand
With powerful grace, that flowed between body and brain
In one unbroken stream, while he stood still there,
Or played even then with the shepherdesses on the swing.

And you here, walking down the street in Houston,
Going to school, what will you do to test your powers?
You are a young god, perhaps, but you will have to learn
With ever more intent precision, how to split into fractions,
And raise to the millionth, holding all in mind, in balance;
And then returning to yourself, rest in your own untroubled
    body.

South, Southwest

Justice is bright; the State is luminous;
Who cannot see the dome flooded with light?
Glowing, almost translucent, like alabaster
Tonight—hardly a shadow to let us think
It was ever dark, or blunted and twisting—
Walking toward it through the elms, sitting
On benches with its influence overhead.

It is like white salt we come to eat;
Take into our eyes, our thin or thick hides,
Let our spirits lick. This was cattle country,
And now we have come to sit at the dome,
To wait. At midnight the sprays are turned on
That keep the grass green—which touching us
Feel suddenly sweet, but then drive us away

Grabbing up sacks, shaking our wet clothes,
Scrambling surprised. Still the dome does not change:
There it gleams. Only, it is distant again,
As we leave, as we fade toward the town, forgetting
But not wholly; pass the Governor's house
Its pure columns lighted too, like snow
Though it's summer, that slaves hauled the logs for.

But we have a new place! Though in the end
They say we keep our own tastes: Crowded shacks
We can smell our acid sweat in and embrace,
Make love like cats with savage clasp, and so
Multiply. The young break plate glass
Snatch shiny rings that make their eyes wide
And run with them in panic through the streets

From the jangling bell. We are animals.
But who's to tell? We live in a tale
With our opposites, separated yet the same.
Tomorrow it will be day again.
The great dome we came for will be gray.
We'll go in, see what they're giving us.
It was like white salt, what we came for.

The Chancellor

He purses his lips, cross, like a female;
Something does not quite please him today,
Does not disappear. Some person is still there
He was rid of, he thought, in his domain.

With such people, you have to use weapons
To make yourself clear—The least would be
Offended benevolence with a veiled threat of rage.
He meditates, but not long.

He rings for those who do what he thinks—
Though who knows, since his temper is treacherous?—
Who assuage his frowns. That close-clipped bullet head,
Behind it a ghostly wig, now thinks it will kill.

Not literally—Yet this troublesome person said he lied!
"Two of you. Produce a file. I want this settled."
In his rising authority he is really like a man.
Past are those days when they laughed that he might be
        chosen.

Yet the cheeks hang in soft folds, though he is hardly old.
And what was this sudden spectacle, of neither strength
Nor charity, against an opponent? He withdraws into him-
        self,
As if already interested in something else.

Hushed, unable to guess, his subordinates hurry out the
   door,
Away from this force that confounds them,
That draws and rejects, and is never distracted from itself:
This thing of unknown sex.

Hardly befitting a song, which should change
All that is wrong into laughter or sorrow
That it is so. Yet with this, neither
Can be told. It has a deadly character.

Famine in Africa

Even the long curving line of pails
Set on the ground, leading to the one well,
Are like fleshless vertebrae, a parched spine;
And the children who cried once are now silent,
Waiting with empty eyes for death,
Great eyes like pails or wells,
Looking at the cracked earth,
The gray crust that cannot feed them,
That is only dry pieces of dust.
Their lips are motionless, as that still line is.

Will even the white people who come be powerless?
Who raise the sheets over their stomachs and look;
Who have always changed the earth.

Chapters for My Faust

I

At first, there was the dream of love.
His soul desired one object;
His will, to give itself completely:

But was scattered among nameless ones,
Slept in strange beds,
Pursued the oblivious dream—
And lay, finally, as one dead:

His soul, remembering,
His will, slowly gathering itself.

II

With impatient rebellion
He said he'd rather play checkers
Than word games with professors.

But he knew within himself,
Though he walked with proud bearing,
How the words haunted his steps—

To prove yourself, whether—

He heard their accent on the stones
His stubborn feet trod,
And when the bells rang out at him.

No laughter, or cleverness,
Or drunken tavern song,
Could drown their echoing.

III

Whose side was he on? None.
He despised their ambitions.
But he knew what losing was,
And though there was Mercy
To win meant life's blood,
Pride, company of men,
That purpose like pure fire
When man and world turn together—
He knew those high moments,
How they rose, and subsided.

Before dawn, one morning,
At Wittenberg he had lain,
Half sleepless, thinking,
1st November, All Hallows—
When he heard reverberate,
Sound from the castle church,
Luther's hammer blows
Nailing up his Protest
On the great wooden door
That would awaken Germany.

For weeks then, crowds in the streets,
Frenzy of liberation,
Matthyszoon who thought he was Gideon,
Bockholdt successor of David,
Munzer who told the peasants
Not to let the blood cool on their swords
All of them—tinker, tailor, shoemaker—
Turned Saviours, butchering,
Themselves butchered in the end.

But the peasants knew not what they did,
The Bishop said, and by the hundreds
Cut off their stupid heads
That had those teachings in them:
To hold all goods in common;
Work, everyone, at a handicraft;
To proceed from these tenets
To the conquest of the world.
At Munster was their center—

Where those three, poor devils,
Knipperdollinck and Krechting
And one John, that had his name,
Had their bodies torn
By the white hot pincers
And were hung in iron cages
Where their sufferings were shown.
It was his own skin there
But for a word the right way.

    Whose side was he on? It was
    Too senseless to determine.

But Luther was a thoughtful man.
When the people clamored in the streets
Demanding that he should speak,
He sent them home sternly.
And the days of Heaven ran out,
Succeeded by an emptiness,
As the long winter began.

    And Jesus took no flesh of the Virgin
    But like water through a pipe—

Toward Christmas, at year's end,
He had left in the falling snow.

IV
What was most beautiful of all?
That the mind could not dispute?

A student's foolish question—

Yet most beautiful of all he knew
Was that summer, walking in the garden,
The woman with her child in her arms,
A radiance surrounding:

                Amidst the leaves,
The flowers, and small quiet animals.

During those years, he learned how grace is given.

Fable

The black, American eagle
Or rather a hawk that now
Plunders the stuffed town

Falls on the squawking turkey,
And the raven that flirts and flutters
Like a comedian with a cane
Or turns to a sad complaint
A burden reiterated—

Devours them both at once
To the last feather and syllable
And spits them together back out,
Ashes on the plowed ground,
On the bare pavement, the asphalt.

Rid of that bitter dose
What transformation occurs?
Crossing the sky now, a dove flies,
And watching, looking up,
He sees, perhaps, a likeness.

At the Pond

Borka it's called, whom by day
Drifting on the water,
The old people watch fondly

As in a sort of dream, a future state,
Feeding it with bread,
For which it stretches its throat

As they are fed still—

Savagely he thinks
He'll end this fantasy,
Seize it and make it choke

Before their very eyes
In broad day;
Or wait till night comes

And do it certainly then.
He can see it waiting there,
White as a spirit in the dark.

He enters the still Park,
And slipping through the shrubs and trees,
Reaches the soft bank;

Pulls off his shirt and pants,
Strikes out toward the swan
Who is tame and sits floating there

Almost asleep; only circling
A bit now, disturbed by him,
Pressing closer to it.

Cutting the black water
He overtakes it easily,
Seizes it in his hands

Clamps it between his arms.
It is amazed like a person,
Or with its wings pinned

Like a sheep it seems, struggling.
It utters a bleating sound.

He pushes it toward the bank,
Drags it up on the grass,
And there unhesitating

Before the watchman can come,
Naked he wrings its neck,
And all those old persons' cries

Silent in the night:
He, with the water dripping
From his legs and chest

At the pond's edge.

The Eagle Has Black Bones—

Suddenly over the page,
Like a stone the words scratched,
The eagle was there, met.

I saw them under the breast
And the feathers of those wings
The shoulders that folded them

And when they were outstretched
And golden to see—still beneath,
Even to the head, the eagle

Was black-boned, inherently.
Even if the wings and breast
Were splattered with black blood

Of sheep or rabbits killed,
They would shake that off.
No, it is his very heart—

Toward which I point the rifle,
Black-barreled, bead of ivory,
That draws him close so his eye

That watches for that heart,
Now looks into mine
In an unbroken line

While the life behind
Beats darkly but steadily
Toward that moment of lightning

When he and I are one
In that murderous flash
When I have struck the heart—

But stopped by the human knowledge,
Or sky I now saw watching;
And the eagle flew, like a shadow.

It is enough to sight.